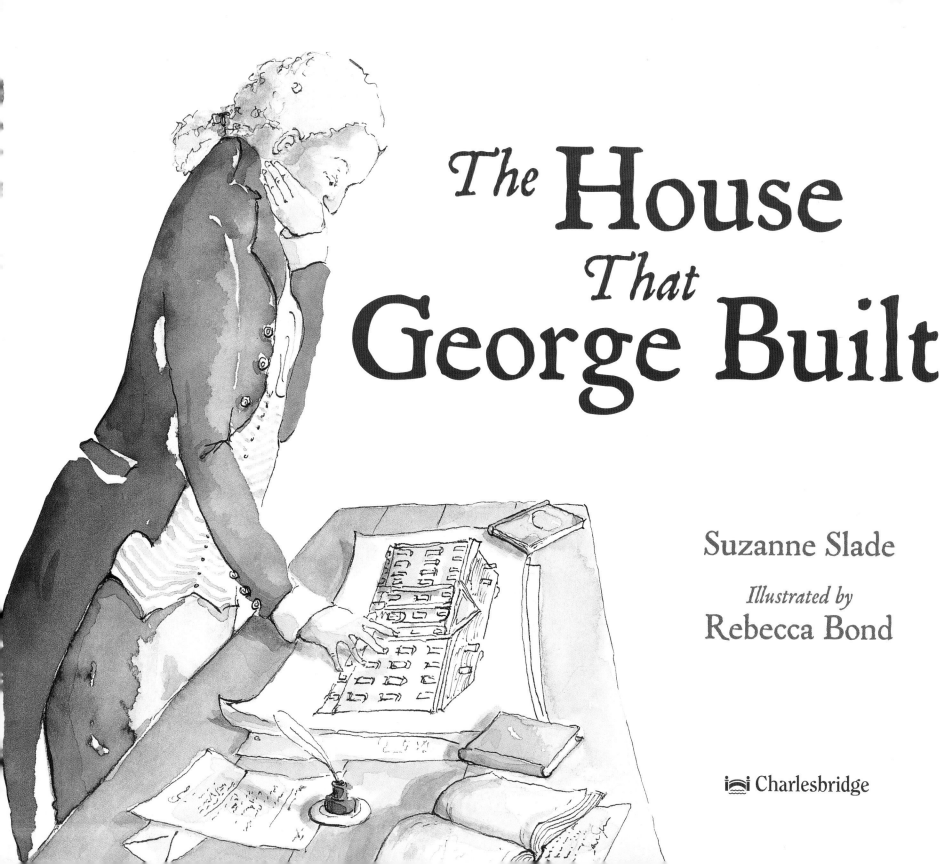

The House That George Built

Suzanne Slade

Illustrated by
Rebecca Bond

Charlesbridge

With love to my parents, George and Martha, who built a wonderful home for our family
—S. S.

For my parents, my sister, and my grandmother, for all your help building my home and my family
—R. B.

Special thanks to William Seale, author of *The President's House: A History* and editor of *White House History*, the journal of the White House Historical Association, for his invaluable expertise and advice.

Published by Charlesbridge
85 Main Street
Watertown, MA 02472
(617) 926-0329
www.charlesbridge.com

Library of Congress Cataloging-in-Publication Data
Slade, Suzanne.
   The house that George built / Suzanne Slade ; illustrated by Rebecca Bond.
      p. cm.
   ISBN 978-1-58089-262-9 (reinforced for library use)
1. White House (Washington, D.C.)—Juvenile literature. 2. White House
(Washington, D.C.)—History—Juvenile literature. 3. Presidents—
United States—History—Juvenile literature. 4. Washington (D.C.)—
Buildings, structures, etc.—Juvenile literature. I. Bond, Rebecca, 1972– ill. II. Title.
F204.W5S65 2011
975.3—dc23   2011025781

Printed in Singapore
(hc) 10 9 8 7 6 5 4 3 2

Illustrations done in watercolor and ink on watercolor paper
Display type and text type set in P22 Mayflower
   and Adobe Caslon Pro
Color separations by KHL Chroma Graphics, Singapore
Printed and bound September 2012 by Imago in Singapore
Production supervision by Brian G. Walker
Designed by Diane M. Earley

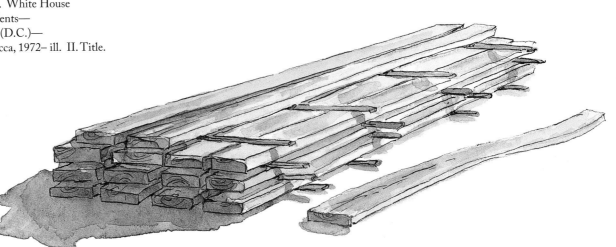

Foreword
(A very short story before the real story)

It all began when the American colonists became
fed up with their English king. They were sick and
tired of his outrageous taxes, unfair rules, and occasional
temper tantrums. So the thirteen colonies fought England
for their freedom. And on July 4, 1776, they formed their
own country—the United States of America.

Now as you might imagine, this new nation didn't want
another bossy, bejeweled king. Instead the people decided
to elect a president. They looked high and low for someone
honest and fair. They searched far and wide for someone
trustworthy and brave.

That someone was George Washington.

George had many responsibilities as the first president. There were laws to pass, important people to meet, and an entire country to run! Although George was the busiest guy in the land, he wanted to create a home where future presidents would live. So George set out to build a special house that would be a symbol of this great new nation.

This is the story
of the President's House
that George built.

First George looked for the perfect place to put this fine house. He searched the land and discovered a beautiful wooded hill in Maryland. On that hill George found a lovely spot overlooking the sparkling Potomac River.

This is the lot,
that grand, scenic spot,

for the President's House that George built.

Next George needed a plan for the President's House. He held a contest and offered $500 or a gold medal to the person with the best design. When the entries started arriving, George got worried. Some drawings were too small and simple for this strong, growing nation. Others were too fussy and frilly for this hardworking, new nation.

Then George spied a magnificent drawing with majestic columns, grand staircases, and a stately oval room. James Hoban's design was just right, and he won the contest.

This is the design,
that would stand for all time,

that was drawn for the lot,
that grand, scenic spot,
for the President's House that George built.

Even though George held the most important job in America, he didn't think he was too important to lend a hand to the building project. George strapped on his boots and helped survey and measure the construction site. Then he pounded in wood stakes to mark the exact location where the President's House would be built.

A large hole was dug between the stakes and filled with stone, wood, and sand, creating a firm foundation for the President's House.

This is the foundation,
that was dug for our nation,

that held the design,
that would stand for all time,
that was drawn for the lot,
that grand, scenic spot,
for the President's House that George built.

Now George needed bricks—lots of them. But how could he get thousands of heavy bricks up the steep hill? Fortunately the mud beneath George's feet contained clay and sand—the perfect ingredients for making bricks! Soon two kilns were baking up red-hot bricks around the clock. Bricklayers used the fresh bricks to lay straight, sturdy walls.

This is the brick,
that was baked strong and thick,

that was laid on the foundation,

that was dug for our nation,

that held the design,

that would stand for all time,

that was drawn for the lot,

that grand, scenic spot,

for the President's House that George built.

Then George faced another problem. The nearby quarries didn't have enough stone to cover the outside of the President's House. He knew there was plenty of beautiful, smooth stone in England, but he would never crawl back to the king! So George changed the house plan from three stories to two, so it would need less stone.

Stoneworkers carved flowers, leaves, and ribbons in the soft sandstone. Then the stone was painted with a thick sealer made of water, lime, salt, glue, and ground-up rice, which turned the house white.

This is the stone,
that was chiseled and honed,

that went over the brick,
that was baked strong and thick,
that was laid on the foundation,
that was dug for our nation,
that held the design,
that would stand for all time,
that was drawn for the lot,
that grand, scenic spot,
for the President's House
that George built.

Progress on the President's House was slow, but George wasn't discouraged. Carpenters built a wooden frame for the roof. They hammered sturdy timbers to support the inside walls. By now over one hundred workers—free men and slaves—lived on the construction site in small, temporary huts. They labored from sunrise till sunset, six long days a week. Busy with presidential duties and the house, George worked seven.

This is the wood,
that was sturdy and good,

that was nailed near the stone,

that was chiseled and honed,

that went over the brick,

that was baked strong and thick,

that was laid on the foundation,

that was dug for our nation,

that held the design,

that would stand for all time,

that was drawn for the lot,

that grand, scenic spot,

for the President's House that George built.

Before George knew it eight years had gone by. The President's House was nearly finished, and so was his time in office. During George's last year as president, building officials asked him to change the plans because the house was getting too expensive. George approved their request to use slate instead of lead for the roof. So the President's House was topped with slate rock. Unfortunately this heavy roof leaked when it rained!

This is the roof,
that was almost waterproof,

that went over the wood,

that was sturdy and good,

that was nailed near the stone,

that was chiseled and honed,

that went over the brick,

that was baked strong and thick,

that was laid on the foundation,

that was dug for our nation,

that held the design,

that would stand for all time,

that was drawn for the lot,

that grand, scenic spot,

for the President's House that George built.

George's term as president ended in 1797. He moved back home to Virginia, where he spent time with his family until his death in 1799. Sadly, George didn't live to see the second president, John Adams, move into the President's House on November 1, 1800. Although the house wasn't completely finished—the plaster walls were still wet, and the winding staircase had only a few steps—John and his wife, Abigail, made it their home.

This is the day,
that John came to stay,
under the roof,
that was almost waterproof,
that went over the wood,
that was sturdy and good,
that was nailed near the stone,
that was chiseled and honed,
that went over the brick,
that was baked strong and thick,
that was laid on the foundation,
that was dug for our nation,
that held the design,
that would stand for all time,
that was drawn for the lot,
that grand, scenic spot,
for the President's House
   that George built.

Many neighbors stopped by to welcome John and Abigail, but most really came to sneak a peek at their incredible home!

This is the house that George built.

The Changing President's House

A lot has happened since John and Abigail Adams moved into the President's House. During the War of 1812, the British set fire to the house. Although much of it burned, it was soon rebuilt to its original splendor. In the years that followed, many presidents made additions to the house that George built. This grand home now has 132 rooms (35 are bathrooms), 412 doors, 28 fireplaces, 8 staircases, and 3 elevators. The President's House was officially renamed the White House by President Theodore Roosevelt in 1901.

✦ James K. Polk installed bright gaslights in 1848 so he could read at night without lighting a candle.

✦ In 1850 Millard Fillmore's wife, Abigail, created a cozy library on the second floor of the President's House.

✦ In 1878 Rutherford B. Hayes planted hundreds of beautiful shade trees on the presidential lawn.

✦ Theodore Roosevelt, who loved to play tennis, added an outdoor tennis court in 1902.

✦ William Howard Taft was the first president to own an automobile. He had the horse stables made into a four-car garage in 1909.

✦ Calvin Coolidge found public life as president very tiring. In 1927 he and his wife, Grace, built a sunny solarium on the roof, where they could rest in privacy.

✦ Franklin D. Roosevelt suffered from polio. Swimming helped ease his discomfort, so children across the country raised money to build him a heated indoor pool in 1933.

✦ Roosevelt also loved movies but found it difficult to get out to a theater. In 1942 he built his own private large-screen movie theater.

✦ A bowling alley was built in 1948 as a birthday present for Harry S. Truman.

✦ Bill Clinton added a hot tub and jogging track to the presidential grounds in 1993.

✦ Barack Obama and his wife, Michelle, like fresh, tasty food. They planted a vegetable garden with fifty-five different vegetables (but no beets—the president doesn't like them!) on the south lawn in 2009.

Author's Note

Soon after George Washington became president in 1789, leaders of the newly formed United States decided to create a capital city with meeting halls, buildings for Congress, and a home for the president. They set a deadline for the President's House to be completed by November 1, 1800. And George wanted it finished on time!

George selected the location for the house so it would have a spectacular view of the Potomac River. This spot was also ideal because it was easy to transport building materials and people along the river. Having worked as a land surveyor, George helped survey the lot, along with Andrew Ellicott and Benjamin Banneker, two men hired to survey the land for the entire city.

In 1791 George invited a French-born architect to design the President's House. Pierre-Charles L'Enfant drew up a plan for a presidential palace, but his ideas were too elaborate and expensive. So George decided to hold a design contest instead. Thomas Jefferson (the future third president) submitted a drawing in the contest under the fake name "AZ." No one figured out Thomas was the mysterious AZ for more than one hundred years! Although George received only nine entries, he was pleased with the design by James Hoban, an immigrant from Ireland. After declaring James the winner, George immediately began helping him improve the design.

While the President's House and capital city were under construction, the government operated out of temporary offices in Philadelphia, Pennsylvania. George lived and worked in Philadelphia, so he chose James to be the on-site construction supervisor of the President's House. James knew the design well and was an experienced supervisor, but whenever he ran into problems, he went straight to George for help. When a stone shortage arose, George changed the design from three stories to two. When money became tight George decided to use wood for the floors instead of expensive marble. Throughout the project George kept in contact with James and visited the construction site whenever his schedule allowed.

The job site turned into a village of laborers living in small huts. Workers skilled in stone, brick, and carpentry, most of them immigrants from Scotland and Ireland, helped with the President's House. Slaves, hired from their owners, and free black men also worked on the immense construction project.

In his last year in office, George continued working hard to make sure the President's House stayed on schedule. He agreed to several cost-saving changes (such as the slate roof) to keep the project within budget. George's dream came true when John Adams moved in on November 1, 1800—right on schedule (although the leaky slate roof wasn't replaced with waterproof sheets of iron until 1804).

For seventy years the President's House was the largest home in the United States. This amazing building took over eight years to finish and ended up costing $272,372 (about $4.9 million today). In honor of George's faithful leadership, the capital city was named after him—Washington, DC. Ironically, every US president except George has lived in the house that George built.

Sources

Burros, Marian. "Obamas to Plant Vegetable Garden at White House." *New York Times,* March 19, 2009. http://www.nytimes.com/2009/03/20/dining/20garden.html.

Caroli, Betty Boyd. *Inside the White House.* New York: Canopy Books, 1992.

"Echoes from the White House: The Changing White House, 1792–1817." PBS. http://www.pbs.org/wnet/whitehouse/timeline/1792.html.

Harris, Bill. *The White House.* Philadelphia: Courage Books, 2002.

Johnson, Paul. *George Washington.* New York: HarperCollins, 2005.

Junior League of Washington. *The City of Washington: An Illustrated History.* Edited by Thomas Froncek. New York: Alfred A. Knopf, 1977.

"Presidential Transitions: 'The Torch Is Passed.'" The White House Historical Association. http://www.whitehousehistory.org/04/subs/04_a03_a01.html.

Seale, William. *The President's House: A History.* Vol. 1. Washington, DC: White House Historical Association, 1986.

Seale, William. *The White House: The History of an American Idea.* Washington, DC: American Institute of Architects Press, 1992.

"White House History." VisitingDC.com. http://www.visitingdc.com/white-house/white-house-history.htm.

Resources to Learn More

Aaseng, Nathan. *The White House.* San Diego, CA: Lucent Books, 2001.

Firestone, Mary. *The White House.* Minneapolis, MN: Picture Window Books, 2007.

Karapetkova, Holly. *The White House.* Vero Beach, FL: Rourke Publishing, 2009.

Our White House: Looking In, Looking Out. Cambridge, MA: Candlewick, 2008.

Rinaldo, Denise. *White House Q & A.* New York: HarperCollins, 2008.

Silate, Jennifer. *The White House.* New York: PowerKids Press, 2006.

The Changing White House
http://www.pbs.org/wnet/whitehouse/timeline/1792.html

A Tour of the White House
http://www.whitehousehistory.org/whha_tours/whitehouse_tour/00.html

The White House Historical Association
http://www.whitehousehistory.org/

The White House Time Machine
http://www.whitehousehistory.org/whha_shows/whitehouse_timemachine/index.htm

The Working White House
http://www.whitehousehistory.org/whha_exhibits/working_whitehouse/